TABLE OF CONTENTS

BONUS MATERIALS

DAY 1

WELCOME TO THIS 30-DAY DEVOTIONAL AND
GenerosityPledge.org
Movement

*This devotional is designed for DAILY personal or family use.
For couples/families, take turns reading sections out loud and talk about what you
read. For groups using this devotional, watch the short videos at GenerosityPledge.org
and use the weekly questions on pages 63-66 to help guide your group discussions.*

Dear Christian friend:

All of us know that it is natural for parents to want their children to learn to be grateful, generous, and giving.

In the same way, our heavenly Father desires his children to become generous and to learn to share whatever they have, whether it is little or much. God desires us to be grateful for what he provides, and he wants us to learn to be open-handed with whatever he gives us.

Unfortunately, in our modern world, many people struggle with materialism, consumerism, indebtedness, concerns about their finances, or fear about what might happen in the future. And in recent years, difficult economic times have challenged people everywhere. But according to the Bible teachings of the prophet Haggai, God sometimes allows cold economic winds to blow to get our attention so that we will "give careful thought to our ways" and rediscover the importance of putting God first in our lives and first in our finances. God wants us to discover afresh how living a life of giving, not just getting, leads us to real joy, lasting happiness, and true contentment.

I started the **GenerosityPledge.org** movement and wrote this devotional because all of us need helpful and encouraging reminders to live generously and to understand that God is our true provider.

During the coming 30 days, the daily devotional readings will focus each day on one of the *7 Keys* in learning to live a generous, open-handed life.

7 KEYS

1. **SUBMIT** yourself and all you have to the LORD
2. **STUDY** the Scriptures on finances and generosity
3. **SEE** what God has provided in your life
4. **SET ASIDE** resources to give
5. **SYSTEMATICALLY** give
6. **SPONTANEOUSLY** give as the LORD leads you
7. **SIMPLIFY** your life to be even more generous.

It is my prayer that God will use this 30-Day Devotional in your personal life and family to bring more joy, contentment, peace, provisions, and wisdom to your life and finances than you ever dreamed was possible.

May God bless you as you begin this journey with an open heart, open mind, and open hands to receive all God has for you.

Yours for inspiring greater generosity and open-handed living everywhere,

Brian Kluth

PASTOR BRIAN KLUTH
Founder of the **GenerosityPledge.org** Movement & **GiveWithJoy.org**
Bestselling author of books at **GodIsYourProvider.com**,
MyFamilyOrganizer.org, and **MAXIMUMgenerosity.org**

DAY 2
First things first

Their first action was to give themselves to the Lord.

When asked to picture a generous person, most of us usually think of someone rich who has excess money, material resources, or time. We might even think to ourselves, "If someday I had some extra, then I would be generous, too. But right now, I have to concentrate on taking care of myself."

The Macedonian Christians were going through very difficult times. They were extremely poor and yet were very generous people. The Bible says of them, in 2 Corinthians 8:2, "Out of the most severe trial, their overflowing joy and their extreme poverty welled up in rich generosity".

What was their secret to becoming joyful and generous people even when they had so little? It started when they first gave themselves to the Lord.

Sometimes people think it is money, education, upbringing, social standing, or religion that makes someone generous. No, these things are not the major reasons people become generous. There are many people who have some or all of these things and have not yet learned to be generous.

To learn to become generous like the Macedonian Christians, we must first give ourselves fully to the Lord. This will help us understand that all we are and all we have comes from the Lord and belongs to the Lord. We will then begin to see God as the true owner of our life and resources. We will see ourselves as the faithful managers of what God entrusts to us. We will then truly begin to realize God's calling on our lives to joyfully and generously share with others whatever he has entrusted to us, whether it is little or much.

SUBMIT yourself and all you have to the LORD

30,000 wallets

Several years ago, I had the privilege of preaching to over 30,000 men at two separate Christian events about what the Bible says about money and living generously. Other speakers at these events often invited the men to come forward at the end of their message to dedicate themselves to Christ. When I came to the end of my message, I took a different approach. Instead of inviting the men to come forward, I asked them to reach into their pockets, take out their wallets and hold them up. If they didn't have a wallet, I asked them to hold up their empty hands. I then led them in the following prayer to dedicate themselves and all they had to God: "Heavenly Father, all I am and all I will ever have comes from you. From this day forward, help me to faithfully manage and generously share my life and resources for your glory for the rest of my life. In Jesus' name, Amen." For many, this was an important step in helping them make the spiritual connection between their wallets and their true worship of God.

SOURCE: www.GiveWithJoy.org - True Generosity Stories

REFLECT/ DISCUSS

Why do you think giving yourself to God is the most important step in learning to become a generous person?

PRAYER

Heavenly Father, we acknowledge you are the owner and we are the managers of what you entrust to us. Help us to live for you each day and to generously share the time, talents, treasures, and things you have given us. AMEN

DAY 3
True financial freedom

ROM 15:4 *Everything that was written in the past was written to teach us.*

If you asked the average person what true financial freedom would look like for them, they would probably give you a number. This number would likely be how much money they believe they would need to make each year, or an amount they would want to have in the bank or invested, to feel "financially free".

But do you know that many people who have lots of money don't feel financially free at all? Instead, they are fearful of losing what they have.

Do you know what TRUE financial freedom looks like? True financial freedom = *your willingness to learn and build your life on biblical financial teachings and to trust God to guide you and provide for you all the days of your life.* Anyone can have this type of financial freedom regardless of whether they have zero dollars or thousands!

To experience this true financial freedom, intentionally search out, read, study, think about, and apply God's Word on finances and generosity in your life. This devotional is a great resource to help you on your journey to financial freedom and to learn to generously live open-handed in a tight-fisted world.

God gave us more than 2000 verses in the Bible on finances, generosity, and material possessions. He gave us all of these verses to teach us how he wants us to feel, think, and act when it comes to money and material possessions. When we begin to read God's Word on finances, any fears we have in our hearts over finances can be replaced with faith in God to be our true provider. God's promises and principles found in the Bible will begin to guide our daily thoughts and financial decisions and we will begin to experience true financial freedom.

The B.I.B.L.E. stands for "Basic Instructions Before Leaving Earth"

Author Unknown

TV news story: "Does God want you rich?"

After the *40-Day Journey to a More Generous Life* Bible devotional became an unexpected bestseller, I was contacted by NBC TV. They wanted to do a news story. When the TV reporter interviewed me, she asked, "So, do you think God wants everyone rich?" I replied, "No, I don't believe that." She was a little surprised by my answer and then asked, "Well, what do you believe?" I responded, "I believe that everyone needs to learn to become more generous with whatever God has given them." Because the 40-day devotional shares 400 Bible verses on finances and generosity, hundreds of thousands of copies have been distributed worldwide by thousands of churches in more than 40 different languages. Why? Because every Christian on the planet needs to learn that God's Word has insights and answers on how they can manage their finances and live generously with whatever God has given them.

SOURCE: www.GiveWithJoy.org - True Generosity Stories

REFLECT/DISCUSS

If someone asked you how much money you would need to have financial freedom, what amount would you have said? Why would learning to look to God as your true provider be more valuable than lots of money in the bank?

PRAYER

Heavenly Father, help us to learn your Word on finances and generosity and to trust you to guide us and provide for us all the days of our lives. AMEN

DAY 4
Paychecks and provisions

1 CHR. 29 :14 | *Everything comes from you, and we have given you only what comes from your hand.*

King David understood God is our provider. He understood each provision we receive comes from God and each gift we give back *to* him first came *from* him.

As a guest speaker at churches and conferences, I will often ask people to raise their hands if they receive a pay check. I then remind everyone that whoever gives them their paycheck is not their provider but their employer. God is their true provider. God can use an employer to help provide for some of our needs, but fortunately, God is much bigger than our employer.

Think about it. What would you rather have in life—only what an employer can pay you or all God can provide for you? God is so much bigger than a pay check, pension, job position, the stock market, and even a country's entire economy. So, while God will often use an employer to help provide for us, his provision is not limited to what a company can pay us.

God can use many different ways to provide for us—our paycheck, bonuses, unexpected cash, extra work, gifts, people's help and hospitality, yard or garage sales, discount prices, savings, investments, pensions, government monies, insurance, and so many other things. All of this can be part of God's provision in our life from the hand of our loving heavenly Father.

When we fully understand God provides in different ways, it will move our hearts from fear to faith as we understand God is bigger than our pay checks. When we learn to truly see the many different ways God provides, we can also learn to joyfully give "thank offerings" to the Lord for his gracious and generous provisions in our life.

God provides a family vacation

A company is not our provider, they are our employer. God is our true provider.

Brian Kluth,
Author &
Speaker

When my wife was nearing the end of her eight-year cancer journey, we decided to take a family vacation while she was still strong enough to travel. I figured that the trip was going to cost thousands, but I knew it would be an important time for our family. When I booked the airline tickets, it turned out I was able to get four frequent flyer tickets, saving over $1000. When I was getting ready to book our hotel, a friend contacted me and offered the use of a furnished apartment she owned near the ocean. When I was about to reserve the rental car, a friend who heard we were coming to town offered us the use of his convertible since he was going to be out of town. Upon arriving, another friend put a $100 bill in my hand and told me to do something nice for my kids. Someone else got us free tickets to Disneyland. I thought the trip was going to cost thousands, but God provided in other amazing ways. So, as a thank offering to the Lord for his provisions, we gave several hundred dollars to a ministry in Africa.

SOURCE: www.GiveWithJoy.org - True Generosity Stories

REFLECT/DISCUSS

If God is truly bigger than a paycheck, what are some ways you have seen him bring provisions into your life recently?

PRAYER

Heavenly Father, open our eyes to "see" your provisions in our life. Help us to acknowledge your financial blessings by giving thank offerings for what you have given us. AMEN

DAY 5
Seven days of God's provisions

1 COR. 16:2 *On the first day of every week, each one of you should put aside money as you have been blessed.*

In Matthew 6:11, Jesus tells us to pray to our heavenly Father for our daily bread. But in 1 Corinthians 16:2, Paul adds to that by reminding us to once a week "look back" over the last seven days to see how and what God has provided. Paul then instructs us to put aside money to give to the Lord's work based on the financial blessings God has provided for us over the past week.

I believe the daily asking, the weekly looking back, and the weekly putting aside of money to give, is truly God's desire for each of us.

By learning to pray to God for our daily bread, we remind ourselves who is the real source for all of our provisions. Looking back each week helps us see the many ways God has provided. Putting money aside helps us to give thanks for God's provision and allows us to joyfully share with others part of what he has given us.

If you begin this weekly practice of "counting your blessings" you will discover that any regular income you receive is only part of God's financial provision and blessing in your life. He can also bless you with things people do for you or give you, food or meals someone shares with you, unexpected financial blessings he provides for you, and savings on things you purchase. The truth is God can provide for you in myriad ways. But only by looking back week by week will you learn to see what God has truly done for you. This will lead to gratefulness in your heart and a growing desire to be more generous. By setting aside offering monies based on your weekly blessings, you will learn to joyfully and willingly share with others some of God's blessings in your life.

SET ASIDE resources to give

4

Count your blessings

As a young married couple, my wife and I had a very small income. We were faithfully giving 10% of our little paycheck to the Lord's work, but we had a growing desire to be even more generous. With such a small pay check, it seemed impossible. I then came across 1 Corinthians 16:2 that implied we should *"count our blessings"* each week and then give offerings to the Lord's work based on what he provided for us. So, on Sunday nights, we began to take out a notebook and write down God's provisions from the past seven days. We discovered God was blessing us and had provided for us in many different ways. So, in addition to giving 10% of our normal paycheck to our local church, we started a "Blessings Fund" to help ministries, missionaries, and the needy. Within 12 months this allowed us to joyfully more than double the amount of money we were giving while still living on a very small salary. We truly discovered God was bigger than a pay check and he had many ways he could provide for us so we could become generous givers.

SOURCE: www.GiveWithJoy.org - True Generosity Stories

REFLECT/DISCUSS

How do you think looking back each week, writing down all of God's provisions, and setting aside money as a thank-you offering to God would help you be more generous?

PRAYER

Heavenly Father, help me learn your Word on finances and generosity and to trust you to guide me and provide for me all the days of my life. AMEN

DAY 6
Giving 10% - no idle suggestion

GEN. 28:20-22 *Jacob made a vow, saying, "If God will be with me and will watch over me…then the Lord will be my God…and of all that you give me I will give you a tenth."*

Jacob left home as a young man with no money in his pocket and an uncertain future. Yet he made a vow to give 10% of anything he received from God.

The Salvation Army's world leader, General Linda Bond, tells a story about learning to give to God. Linda, a Canadian, moved from her home in Nova Scotia to Winnipeg, Manitoba and needed to find a job. The Lord called her to be a Salvation Army officer, and she had to save money for the two-year training period. The relocation meant she needed to live with her oldest sister's family. Finding work wasn't hard for Linda but earning a decent salary was. She needed every cent she could get. But then her sister reminded her that salary earners in her house tithe (give 10% to God). Tithe? Well, if you knew Linda's sister you would know this was no idle suggestion. It was the rule of the house. From that day forward, giving 10% became the norm for Linda. Offerings and sacrificial gifts were the extras on top of the 10%. By doing this, she knew she was helping God's work and being a faithful Christian.

In recent years, she read the *40-Day Spiritual Journey to a More Generous Life* Bible devotional. She said in a magazine article this devotional brought her face-to-face with the difference between what someone gives and what they could give. It was the difference between obligation and generosity. It moved her from asking how much she should give to how much she should keep.

Like Jacob and Linda, learning to give to God is part of our spiritual journey with important milestones along the way.

SYSTEMATICALLY give

Young man in debt writes the first check to God

> *Giving 10% isn't the finish line of giving, it's the starting blocks.*
>
> Randy Alcorn,
> Author

After I finished school and began working, I signed up for some credit cards. With the "help" of my credit cards, I soon learned how to follow the "see-it, like-it, charge-it, and figure-out-how-to-pay-for-it-later" plan. I quickly had more month than money. One day I sat at my desk with a small paycheck, empty check book, and a big pile of bills to pay. I looked at the mess I had created and knew I was in trouble. Suddenly, there was a desire in my heart to write the first check to God's work–a 10% tithe. What? Give 10%? Am I crazy? I don't have enough now. If I give 10% I will have even less!

But I knew God was calling me to trust him. With a shaking hand, I wrote the first 10% check to God. I then prayed for wisdom on what to pay next and how to get by until my next pay check. God was faithful. He helped me continue to give while guiding me to become debt-free within two years. God taught me that little becomes much when God is in it.

SOURCE: www.GiveWithJoy.org - True Generosity Stories

REFLECT/DISCUSS

What are some of the most vivid recollections you have about your personal giving or your family's giving to God?

PRAYER

Heavenly Father, help us to overcome our fears about giving with an expectant faith in your ability to provide. AMEN

DAY 7
A little boy's lunch
is more than enough

JOHN 6:9

Andrew, Simon Peter's brother, spoke up, "Here is a boy with five small barley loaves and two small fish, but how far will they go among so many?" Jesus said, "Have the people sit down."

Jesus had been teaching thousands of people in a deserted place outside of town. It was well past the dinner hour, and people were getting hungry. Jesus told his disciples to feed everyone. They looked at their empty money bag and quickly informed Jesus there was no way they had enough money to buy enough food to feed everyone. And even if they did, they weren't near a town. There wasn't anywhere they could buy food. Then Andrew spoke up and said a little boy had come forward and wanted to give Jesus all the food he had to help feed the crowd. The five loaves and two fish were probably what his mother packed for him before he had excitedly run out of the house to try and see Jesus. The little boy wanted to be part of the big crowd going by his house.

Jesus took what the little boy spontaneously offered, gave thanks for it, miraculously multiplied it, and gave it to his disciples to feed thousands of hungry people.

The disciples were professing believers but practicing atheists when it came to their willingness to believe God could take little and make it into much. The little boy, on the other hand, had complete confidence this miracle-working Jesus could take whatever he gave and multiply it to miraculously help others.

It is good to be reminded that no matter how impossible some situations seem, if we offer whatever we have to Jesus, he can take it and use it to bless us and many others.

SPONTANEOUSLY give as the LORD leads you

Little girl's 57 pennies

Hattie May Wiatt was a young girl who lived near a growing church in Philadelphia in the 1880s. One day, Hattie was found crying because there was not enough room in the Sunday School for her to attend. Pastor Conwell placed her on his shoulders and carried her through the waiting crowds into the church. She began saving her pennies to help build a larger Sunday School. She had saved 57 cents (which was a lot of money back then) when she became sick and died. Hattie May's parents gave the little purse with the 57 pennies in it to Pastor Conwell. They told him Hattie had been saving the money to help buy a bigger Sunday School building. The 57 pennies were auctioned off and grew to $250. This money was used as the down payment to help buy a building next door to the church. Hattie May Wiatt's picture is still hanging in this building. The first college class of what is now Temple University was also started in this building (and Temple has educated more than 80,000 students over the years). The church also started the Wiatt Mite Society to continue expanding her 57 cents to support the Lord's work. This all happened because of the generosity and sacrifice of one little girl who saved and gave 57 pennies.

SOURCE: *Igniting a Life of Generosity* devotional

REFLECT/DISCUSS

Why do you think God can use the faith of little children to accomplish big things for God's glory? Why is it important for you to cultivate childlike faith in your giving?

PRAYER

Heavenly Father, help us to understand that "little can become much" when you are in it. AMEN

DAY 8
How much is enough?

PROV. 30:8 *Give me neither poverty nor riches!*
Give me just enough to satisfy my needs.

Have you ever thought about "how much is enough"? One wealthy person was asked this question and he answered, "Just a little bit more." But this isn't the picture Scripture paints. The writer of Proverbs 30:8 was inspired by the Holy Spirit to pray for enough to satisfy his needs (not his "greeds"). How much would be enough to meet your real needs? If God provided you with extra beyond this amount, how could you use the extra for the glory of God and the benefit of others?

Part of the process of discovering how much is enough is to determine the difference between your needs and wants. I believe God is concerned about our real needs and often graciously provides for desires. But he is not a magic genie in a bottle who gives us three wishes so we can have everything we set our eyes on.

In my own family, I was more materialistic than my wife. She was a very content person and did not seek after lot of extra things. Her contentment and wisdom frequently protected us from buying things we didn't really need. The problem for many of us is we think contentment comes from getting everything we want. But the truth is real contentment comes from being thankful for everything we have and sharing it with others.

1 Timothy 6:8 tells us that godliness with contentment is great gain. Any of us, regardless of our age or income, can have great gain if we love Jesus, follow him, and are thankful and generous with everything he has given us. Once we realize we can be "content" with God and his provisions, we can then pray and ask God to show us what enough is. Once we know what enough is, we can then joyfully share any of the over-and-above resources we receive for the glory of God and the benefit of others.

SIMPLIFY your life to become more generous

The tale of two checkbooks

Sometimes God increases our income not to increase our standard of living but to increase our standard of giving.

Randy Alcorn,
Author

A number of years ago, I was inspired by a young businessman and his wife who prayerfully decided they would live on his $50,000 annual salary and give any additional income to God's work. Within six years, they had given over $1 million! I was so moved by this story I talked with my wife about doing something similar. We decided to open up a second checkbook. The first account would be our *"living"* checkbook and the second one would be our *"giving"* checkbook. We determined a specific five figure income that would be "enough" to put into our living checkbook each year, and everything else would flow into our giving checkbook. Since then, we have been happy and content "living" on five figures, and have joyfully used five or six figures every year from the giving checkbook for God's work. Our giving checkbook has allowed us to give special gifts to our church, ministries, missions, charities, and the needy. We have also used money in the giving checkbook to **create** generosity materials being used around the world—including this devotional!

SOURCE: www.GiveWithJoy.org - True Generosity Stories

REFLECT/DISCUSS

Would you be willing to pray and, with God's help, determine how much is "enough"? If God gave you extra money beyond this amount, how would you want to use it for God's work?

PRAYER

Heavenly Father, help us to determine what "enough" is for our family and to joyfully and generously share the rest. AMEN

DAY 9
The tale of two young men

MATT 10:39 *If you cling to your life, you will lose it; but if you give up your life for me, you will find it .*

Here are some valuable insights from Randy Alcorn's blog: The streets of Cairo, Egypt were hot and dusty. Our missionary friends took us down an alley. We drove to a gate that opened to a plot of overgrown grass. It was a graveyard for American missionaries. We saw a tombstone that read— William Borden, 1887-1913.

Borden, a Yale graduate and heir to great wealth, rejected a life of ease in order to bring the gospel to others. Borden gave away hundreds of thousands of dollars to missions. After only four months of ministry in Egypt, he became sick and died at the age of 25. I dusted off the epitaph on Borden's grave which ended with a phrase I've never forgotten: "Apart from faith in Christ, there is no explanation for such a life."

We then went to the King Tut exhibit and it was mind-boggling. Tutankhamen, the boy king, was only 17 when he died. His burial site was filled with valuable treasure and tons of gold.

I was struck by the contrast between these two graves. Borden's was obscure, dusty and hidden off the back alley of a street littered with garbage. King Tut's tomb glittered with unimaginable wealth. Yet where are these two young men now? One, who lived in opulence and called himself king, is in the misery of a Christ-less eternity. The other, who lived his life in service of the one true King, is enjoying his everlasting reward in the presence of his Lord. Tut's life was tragic because of an awful truth discovered too late—he couldn't take his treasure with him. William Borden's life was triumphant. Why? Because instead of leaving behind his treasure, he sent it on ahead.

SUBMIT yourself and all you have to the LORD

Millionaire to missionary

He is no fool who gives what he cannot keep to gain that which he cannot lose.

Jim Elliot,
Martyred Missionary
to South America
1927-1956

In 1904, William Borden graduated from high school at the age of 16. As heir to the Borden family fortune, he was a very wealthy man. During an around-the-world graduation trip, God put a desire in Borden's heart to become a missionary. Borden attended college at Yale and a fellow student wrote, "He came to college far ahead, spiritually, of any of us. He had already given his heart in full surrender to Christ." During college, Borden made an entry in his journal that simply said, "Say 'no' to self and 'yes' to Jesus every time." Borden and a friend started a college ministry that eventually grew to 1300 students that would meet for prayer and Bible study before breakfast. He also ministered to widows, orphans, and the needy. After attending Princeton Seminary, Borden left for the mission field. While studying Arabic in Egypt, he became sick and died at the age of 25. In addition to sharing his life and wealth while he was alive, the New York Times reported Borden left nearly his entire estate (~$1 million) to foreign missions and Christian causes.

SOURCE: www.GiveWithJoy.org - True Generosity Stories

REFLECT/DISCUSS

Why do you think money and material possessions hold such an attraction for most people? What can you learn from the lives of William Borden and King Tut?

PRAYER

Heavenly Father, help us to live more for eternity than life here on earth. AMEN

DAY 10
Only one thing

The Lord said to her, "My dear Martha, you are so upset over all these details. There is really only one thing worth being concerned about. Mary has discovered it – and I won't take it from her."

What are you concerned about today? School, work, sports, relationships, finances, or family? Every day, there are so many things that can flood our minds and fill our days with anxiety and worry.

Martha had a house full of unexpected company and was trying to get a big meal ready for Jesus and his friends. There was lots to be done and Martha was busy doing it. But instead of helping in the kitchen, her sister, Mary, was sitting at Jesus' feet and listening to what he had to say. The harder Martha worked without Mary's help, the madder she got. Finally she had enough. Martha marched into the room where Mary and others were listening to Jesus and told Jesus to tell Mary to help her. But instead, Jesus said there was only one thing worth being concerned about and it wasn't dinner!

Most people don't spend time reading God's Word when they wake up every morning because they start their day so concerned about the many things they feel they have to do that day. They wake up and enter their day with anxious hearts, troubled minds, stress in their bodies, and pain in their faces.

Like Mary, I discovered many years ago, that I needed to spend time with the Lord. I decided to make the time and take the time every morning and evening to read God's Word and pray. I have found the Lord then gives me the strength, guidance, and wisdom to handle the challenges I face each day. Hopefully, all of us can learn a lot from the story of Mary and Martha about the one thing that is more important.

Psalm $67.07 gift

> *He who runs from God in the morning will scarcely find him the rest of the day.*
>
> John Bunyan,
> Author of
> Pilgrim's Progress,
> 1628-1688

I was having my daily morning devotions when I came across Psalm 67:7, "God blesses us that all the ends of the earth will worship him." Later at work that day, I was given a small bonus. I immediately wondered, "How can I use this financial blessing to help someone at the ends of the earth?" That night, I was talking with a young woman who was going on a mission trip to a small island in the Philippines. Since this was on the other side of the world, it sure sounded like the ends of the earth to me. With Psalm 67:7 still on my mind, I handed her $67.07 and told her when she got to the island that she should find someone that really needed help. I asked her to give the person the $67.07 in cash and Psalm 67:7 written on a card. Several weeks later, I received a letter from a young Filipino man telling he received the money from my friend, and that the money and verse met a great need in his life.

SOURCE: www.GiveWithJoy.org - True Generosity Stories

REFLECT/DISCUSS

1 Peter 5:7 tells us to "cast all of our cares upon him because he cares for us." What is something that is troubling you? How can you better use the time and energy you spend worrying to instead worship God in this matter?

PRAYER

Heavenly Father, forgive us for being so anxious about so many things and not spending more time listening to you. Help us to turn to you and learn from you every day. AMEN

DAY 11
Big offering baskets in India

EX. 35:5 *From what you have, take an offering for the Lord. Everyone who is willing is to bring to the Lord an offering.*

Hundreds of thousands of Israelite slaves left Egypt in the middle of the night under the leadership of Moses.

While they were in the wilderness, God spoke to Moses about building a tabernacle as a center for the people's worship and religious life. God's instructions to the people through Moses were "from what you have, take an offering for the Lord". I love this idea of learning to give from what we have. There is no need to worry, grumble, or complain about what we don't have, but to joyfully and generously give from what we do have. This is true for everyone, regardless of how little we may have.

While a guest preacher at a small mud hut church with a dirt floor in India, it came time to take up the offering. They passed around large plastic wastepaper baskets. Later, I asked the pastor why the baskets were so big. He told me he taught his people to give from "what they have". He showed me one of the baskets. It was filled with rice, bread, eggs, vegetables, fruit and a little bit of money. He went on to say that financially the people were very poor, but they learned to trust God to provide for them and to generously give from whatever he provided for them during the week.

In another church I visited in India, they even built "tithe houses" the size of an average home. These tithe houses were built so people could faithfully bring the first portion of their crops to the Lord's house to support the church's ministries and missions outreach.

God invites each of us to determine what he has provided in our lives. We can then generously share from what we have (our time, talents, treasure, and things) to honor God and help advance his work in our church, community, and world.

SEE what God has provided

Laptop computer for the Bhutan Bible

The Bible teaches we are to give from "whatever we have". While ministering in northeast India, I found myself without any cash. There wasn't an ATM for hundreds of miles. However, all my needs were being met by my hosts. I was introduced to a man from Burma who for 10 years had been translating, by hand, the entire Bible into the Bhutanese language. He had 66 school notebooks filled with his translation work. He now needed a computer so he could type everything into it and have the Bible printed and distributed all over Bhutan. I wanted to help him, but I didn't have any money. The Lord spoke to my heart with the thought, "He doesn't need money, he needs a computer. Give him the laptop you have." I stayed up most of the night transferring my files to an external hard drive. Early the next morning, I gave my laptop to this Christian brother so he could finish his translation work. He left rejoicing in God's provision. A few years later, I received a copy of the Bhutan Bible (see picture) that my laptop helped complete.

SOURCE: www.GiveWithJoy.org - True Generosity Stories

REFLECT/DISCUSS

List some of the available time, talents, treasure, and things that God has given you. What is a way that some of these things could be used for the Lord and for others?

PRAYER

Heavenly Father, help us to clearly see what you have given us and help us to generously and joyfully share it for your glory. AMEN

DAY 12
Three envelopes

LEV. 27:30 *One tenth of the produce of the land, whether grain from the fields or fruit from the trees, belongs to the Lord and must be set apart to him as holy.*

I once heard someone say everyone spends the first 10% of their income somewhere, but the wise people give their first 10% to God to honor him and thank him for his provision in their life.

Think about it. Whenever you get money, it begins to flow out. Sometimes it even flows out faster than it is coming in! But wise people make sure the first tenth—or more—of their financial blessings flows back to God's work. This doesn't happen accidentally, it happens intentionally. And the very best way to do this intentionally is to "set apart" your giving for the Lord's work.

When my children were young, they each had three money envelopes. Whenever they received money for some work they did or as a gift, we would help them set apart 10% into their giving envelope, 20% would go into a savings envelope, and the rest would go in their spending envelope. As parents, we wanted our children to know all they had comes from God, and it was right to honor and thank him for his provision by giving the first 10% or more—back to God.

Do you have a plan to intentionally set aside resources to give to God? I know one elderly woman who set apart God's money in a cookie jar. Another person I know had a separate bank account for the Lord's money. Others give money electronically every month. And some keep a special book-keeping account for their giving. Setting up a plan and starting this practice of being a faithful giver will allow you to give to God whats right, not what's left.

Little girl finds God's money in a drawer

Pat was in her late 80s when she told me a story. When she was seven years old, during the Great Depression, she asked her mother for a penny to buy candy. Her mother replied, "Honey, we don't have a penny." Pat answered, "Mommy, yes we do!" "Where do we have a penny?" Asked her mother. "In that drawer over there." "What do you mean?" "In that drawer there's a little box. We've got over $2 in that box." "Honey, that's God's money. That money doesn't belong to you and that money doesn't belong to us. That's God's." "Where did you get that $2 from, Mommy?" "Well, I went and worked 10 days as a nurse for somebody who was very sick and I got $30. When I came home I put $3 in that little tin, and that's God's money. We gave $1 of it away and now we still have $2 left to give." "What about the rest of the money?" "That's all gone, and we don't have a penny in this house for us." Pat never forgot that lesson. At a very young age, she learned some things belong to God, even when you are facing tough times. May we come to understand the same thing.

SOURCE: www.GiveWithJoy.org - True Generosity Stories

REFLECT/DISCUSS

If you have an intentional plan for setting aside 10% or more of your financial blessings for God's work, what is that plan? If you haven't done this yet, what could you do to start?

PRAYER

Heavenly Father, help us to see your financial blessings in our life and then to have an intentional way to set aside 10% or more to give back to your work. AMEN

DAY 13
Declaring who is #1 in your life

DEUT. 14:23 *The purpose of tithing is to teach you always to put God first in your lives.*

Pastor James MacDonald once wrote: "First things belong to God. The first day of the week belongs to God. The first hour of the day belongs to God. The first portion of your income belongs to God. When you make God first, he will help you."

While we should all realize 100% of our lives, time, and resources belong to God. There is something about systematically honoring him first that brings God's order to all of our finances. In the Old Testament, tithing (giving 10%) was a way for people to declare to God he had the first place in their life and finances. In the New Testament, we are instructed to seek first the kingdom of God, and the things necessary for life will be added to us.

When it comes to starting each day, it is wise to spend time in devotions and prayer. When it comes to our week, it is wise to join together with the family of God at church for worship, teaching, service, and fellowship. When it comes to our financial blessings and provisions, it is wise to give 10% or more to the Lord's work. With each of these actions, we are declaring to God, ourselves, and to anyone watching our lives that following God is the most important thing in the world to us. And when we do this, we find God guides us, provides for us, protects us, and watches over us.

Reading God's Word, praying, worshipping, serving, and giving aren't to be sporadic things in our lives. Instead they are to be a systematic part of what we do and how we live. Declaring God #1 is not just about lip service, but about life service – living for him and honoring him day by day and week by week with all we are and all we have.

Little boy's three jars and $2 gift

I will never forget teaching a Sunday School class of squirming, silly eight-year-old boys. I brought enough jars and labels to the class so each boy could make up three money jars. I was trying to teach them the three primary purposes for money – give, save, live. The first jar was for giving to God, the second for savings, and the third for living/spending. Each boy did a good job designing their labels and putting them on their three jars. I told them whenever they got any money they should divide it between the three jars, always starting with God's jar first. A few months later, I was about to head off on a six-week ministry trip to India and Alex came running up to me at church and pushed two $1 bills into my hand. I asked him, "Alex, what's this for?"

He said, "Teacher, do you remember the three jars? I went home and did what you said. These two $1 bills are from God's jar and you're going to India to do God's work and God wants me to help you. And today I heard about a missionary in Africa, so I am going to start putting more money in God's jar to help him." That morning, I realized Alex got what some people never get—the first purpose of money is to give to God's work.

SOURCE: www.GiveWithJoy.org - True Generosity Stories

REFLECT/DISCUSS

If someone looked over your calendar and financial records, who and what would they say is important to you?

PRAYER

Heavenly Father, help us to live for you each day and each week by giving you first place in our calendar and finances. AMEN

DAY 14
What's in your hand?

EX. 4:2

Then the LORD asked him, "What do you have there in your hand?" "A shepherd's staff," Moses replied..

For 40 years, Moses lived in the desert on the backside of a mountain as a runaway, being a shepherd to his father-in-law's sheep. But when he was 80 years old, he had a personal encounter with God who asked him, "What do you have in your hand, Moses?" "A shepherd's staff," Moses replied. God then told him to throw the staff down and it became a snake. Moses was then told to pick up the snake by the tail, and when he did, it became a shepherd's staff again. When Moses had used the staff for those 40 years as a shepherd, it had been a symbol of his personal power, protection, and provision. But after his encounter with God, it became a symbol of God's miracles in front of the Egyptians and the Israelites.

What's in our hands? What skills, provisions, time, abilities, and resources do we personally possess? What do we lean on as our source of power, protection, and provision? Under God's direction, are we willing to throw these things down? Are we willing to release our control and ownership of these things? And if we do, when God tells us to pick them up, are we willing to use them under the Lord's direction and for his glory?

When we are open to spontaneously releasing everything in our hands to the Lord, we will have the privilege of being part of God miracles for all to see. What may be our prized possessions, proven skills, personal positions of influence, prideful accomplishments, available time, or stored-up resources can become part of a living miracle when we yield whatever is in our hands to be used by the Lord.

SPONTANEOUSLY give as the LORD leads you

Meal-time decision becomes a million dollars for the Lord's work

What makes the Dead Sea dead? It is always taking in, but never giving out.

D.L. Moody,
Evangelist
1837-1899

I know of a couple who decided to sell a beautiful, debt-free, $4 million home they owned. But the house sat quietly on the market for several years with no offers. One day over a meal, the man commented to his wife, "Maybe the reason God hasn't allowed the house to sell yet is we don't know what we'd do with all the money if we did sell it." They decided to write down some things they would like to do with the $4 million. First, they wanted to give over a $1 million to the Lord's work by helping their church, widows and orphans, and missions.

They also wanted to build a retirement home and to be of help to their children. Shortly after, they received a $4 million offer on their house! When the check arrived, they followed through on their commitment to give over $1 million to the Lord. They also continued to serve the Lord faithfully and generously with their time and talents in their local church and other ministries.

SOURCE: www.GiveWithJoy.org - True Generosity Stories

REFLECT/DISCUSS

Whether someone is rich or poor, why do you think possessions become such an attraction and/or distraction for people? Why can't possessions bring lasting happiness?

PRAYER

Heavenly Father, whether we have little or much, help us to always live open-handed in a tight-fisted world and to find our greatest joy in following and serving you. AMEN

DAY 15
Two rich young rulers –
A sad one and a glad one

MATT 19:21 *Jesus told the rich young ruler, "If you want to be perfect, go and sell all your possessions and give the money to the poor, and you will have treasure in heaven. Then come, follow me."*

The Bible tells the story of two rich young rulers in Matthew 19 and I Kings 19. In Matthew 19, we learn of the rich young ruler Jesus loved. Jesus invited him to become one of his followers, but the young man learned he was going to have to "de-accumulate" his wealth and possessions in order to follow the Lord. Jesus knew the young man was not only attracted to possessions but had become distracted by his possessions. Ultimately, the young man decided to cling to his possessions instead of letting them go to follow Jesus.

But in 1 Kings 19, we learn of another rich young ruler. Elisha was part of a very wealthy farming family. When the prophet Elijah came to speak to Elisha, he found him ploughing a field with 12 teams of oxen. A man with one oxen and a field is a farmer, but a man plowing with 24 oxen is a very wealthy farmer with a big business. Elijah called Elisha to leave his business and enter the ministry. The Bible says "Elisha returned to his oxen and slaughtered them. He used the wood from the plough to build a fire to roast their flesh. He passed around the meat to the townspeople and they all ate. Then he went with Elijah as his assistant."

Two wealthy young men had a decision to make. One was distracted by his wealth. One was more attracted to serving God. One wouldn't freely give, blessed no one, and went away sad. One freely let go, blessed others, and became glad. One we never hear about again; one was taken on an amazing lifetime journey of serving God and others.

SIMPLIFY your life to become more generous

Triple car miracle

One morning while I was reading my Bible, the Lord prompted my heart to give my car away! I knew a mom with many young children who was driving an older Suburban which put a strain on her monthly gas budget. I had a station wagon that was only a few years old, and it got good gas mileage. I asked my wife what she thought about giving this family our station wagon, and she liked the idea. We ended up giving this mom our car in exchange for her large SUV. Our family didn't need a big SUV, but we had Christian missionary friends who lived over 1000 miles away who had been praying for this type of vehicle. So, we drove this vehicle the 1000 miles to give it to this missionary family. Now I was without a car! But a good friend of ours in the town we travelled to had an extra car he had been trying to sell for three months to get some cash. The price he wanted was what we could pay for with a personal check. We bought his car and drove home rejoicing how God had allowed us to bless three families – the mom and her children, the missionary's family, and the family that needed to sell its extra car. And our family was blessed to be part of this triple miracle.

SOURCE: www.GiveWithJoy.org - True Generosity Stories

REFLECT/DISCUSS

Name a few of your most prized possessions, proven skills/abilities, available time, or stored-up resources. Have you ever fully yielded these things to God?

PRAYER

Heavenly Father, show us what you have placed in our hands. Help us to use it for your glory for all to see. AMEN

DAY 16
Your bed is your altar

> **ROM 12:1**
>
> *I urge you, brothers and sisters, in view of God's mercy, to offer your bodies as a living sacrifice, holy and pleasing to God—this is your true and proper worship.*

Have you ever seen stone or wood altars in a movie or book? They are usually a rectangular shape about the length of a human being. In many pagan religions, priests would actually put people to death on these altars as a sacrifice to please or appease the pagan gods they worshipped.

The Apostle Paul urges us to offer our bodies not as a one-time human sacrifice, but as a DAILY living sacrifice to God. Our bed can become God's altar! When we open our eyes each morning, this rectangular-shaped altar can be the place where we prayerfully dedicate ourselves and all we have to God's service for that day. We can then go into our day confident God will direct us and use us no matter what happens. If we have dedicated ourselves to God's service, each conversation, each problem, each uncertainty, each need, and each opportunity for doing good becomes a chance to let the love and light of God shine through us to others.

It is true many people around the world are still being martyred for their faith in Christ. And we must all be willing to die for Christ if and when that becomes necessary. But for many of us, the willingness to die for Christ is not nearly as important as our willingness to live for Christ each and every day that God gives us on this planet.

So, on our altar beds each morning, we need to dedicate ourselves, our day, and our things to God. Our daily activities, attitudes, and actions can then allow us to be "Jesus with skin on" to the people around us by showing and sharing God's love with them in personal and tangible ways for the glory of God.

Milk for a prisoner's family

One day I was talking to a young boy whose father was in prison. He was from a large family with lots of young children. Somehow the subject of milk came up in our conversation. The boy mentioned he loved milk, but his family didn't get to drink it very often because they couldn't afford it. The Lord brought to my mind Matthew 10:42 which I had read in my devotions that morning, This verse reminds us whoever gives even a cup of water to a child, God will record, remember, and reward this small act of kindness. I went home and talked with my wife about this family and this verse. We joyfully decided to purchase a year's supply of milk to be delivered to this boy's home every week so their entire family could enjoy milk without their mother having to go out and buy it. We have gladly continued doing this each year. We love this family and have enjoyed seeing God's blessing on their lives in spite of the hardships they have had to go through.

SOURCE: www.GiveWithJoy.org - True Generosity Stories

REFLECT/DISCUSS

The Apostle Paul says we are to live for God each day. Albert Einstein says we are to live for others. How do you think these two things work together, like the wings of a bird in flight?

PRAYER

Heavenly Father, we dedicate all we are and all we have to you on this day as living sacrifices. Help us to show and share your love with others today. AMEN

DAY 17
Brain training

Do not conform to the pattern of this world, but be transformed by the renewing of your mind. Then you will be able to test and approve what God's will is—his good, pleasing and perfect will.

Have you ever heard the phrase, G.I.G.O.? It is a computer programming term that refers to "Garbage In, Garbage Out". If you put bad information into a computer, you will get bad information out of it.

Our brains are like computers. They gather and store a lot of information about thousands of things. But if we only get our information about finances and possessions from the internet, TV, friends, music, movies, news, magazines, billboards, and other worldly sources, we will be getting "garbage in", and we will be squeezed into the world's mold. This "garbage in" will result in "garbage out" in our financial lives. We will make poor financial decisions, impulse purchases, and will waste money chasing after things that really can't bring lasting satisfaction and joy.

God has a better way. He wants us to intentionally train our brains to think his thoughts on finances, giving, and material possessions. His Word can reprogram our brains to experience his thoughts, his will, and his ways in these important areas of our lives. His Word will allow us to be "transformed" as God reprograms our thinking. We will break out of the financial bondage of worldly thinking about financial and giving matters. We will begin to experience God's peace, wisdom, and guidance when it comes to money, things, giving, and sharing. We will then experience true contentment and lasting joy as we discover and follow his good, pleasing and perfect will in our lives.

Firewood for a church in Bulgaria

> *Give according to your income, lest God make your income according to your giving.*
>
> Author unknown

Years ago, I taught a stewardship seminar in Greece to leaders from all over Europe. Nik, from Bulgaria, told me this was the first time he learned that everyone is to give to God from whatever they have, whether it is little or much. When he returned home, a church group asked if he knew any rich people who could give money to help them buy firewood to keep their church warm. Nik asked if they had enough wood to keep their own houses warm and they said yes. He told them that if God had blessed them with firewood, they should bring some of the wood to the church. They replied, "No, we are too poor to give, and the wood we have belongs to us."

Nik continued, "God has already blessed you with the wood you need for your church and your homes, but you need to learn to faithfully give from whatever God has given you!" He gave them the verses on generosity I shared at the seminar. Within weeks, giving began to increase as people brought their wood, garden produce, and money from the blessings God had given them.

SOURCE: www.GiveWithJoy.org - True Generosity Stories

REFLECT/DISCUSS

What are the tangible financial, material, and other provisions God has blessed you with? What is your plan to systematically share these provisions?

PRAYER

Heavenly Father, help us to see and systematically set aside resources to give from the blessings you have given us. AMEN

DAY 18
Generosity = God's crazy math

LUKE 6:38 *Give, and it will be given to you. A good measure, pressed down, shaken together and running over, will be poured into your lap. For with the measure you use, it will be measured to you."*

I have never liked the "prosperity gospel". In many places of the world this greed-based, God-wants-you-rich, and give-to-get teaching has harmed many people. Many proponents of this message have lived extravagant lifestyles while fleecing their flock instead of feeding their flock. I like to remind people that God is interested in meeting our needs, but he isn't interested in our "greeds"!

While I don't like the prosperity gospel, I do believe being generous and giving to God does allow us to experience "God's crazy math". The reason most people don't give is because they are fearful. They feel they don't have enough, and if they give they think they will have even less. But many Christians have discovered that when we learn to give to God, he begins to give us "more". This "more" he gives comes in many different forms. He gives us more wisdom in our finances than we had before we learned to give. He gives us more peace, more contentment, more joy, more courage to make better financial decisions, and more grace to be grateful for his many blessings. God also miraculously stretches the little we have to make it "enough" to meet our real needs.

Without God, giving generously is crazy! But when we seek first the kingdom of God in our lives and finances, our loving heavenly Father graciously guides us, provides for us, and blesses us in many, many ways. Our giving doesn't cause us to have less, but instead allows us to have more of what we really need—God's presence, protection, promises, peace, and provisions.

SEE what God has provided

Cinderella winter boots

When I was in my 20s, I quit my job and joined the missionary staff of a Christian camp in northern Wisconsin. My salary was slashed by 90%, but I had great joy in serving the Lord. Even on this small income, I continued to give first to the Lord. When winter hit and the snow started to accumulate for its six-month stay, I realized I only had city shoes and no warm boots. One morning, I prayed and asked God to send me money so I could buy winter boots. When I checked my mail, I received three letters from friends, but there was no money in the envelopes. I was a bit discouraged, but then my friend, Larry, came into the camp office carrying a pair of winter boots. He asked if anyone needed some warm boots. He had bought a new house that had a barn. In the hay loft, he found some winter boots which weren't his size. I told Larry I needed some boots. When I tried them on, I felt like Cinderella because they were my exact size! That day I learned my heavenly Father's provisions were bigger than money, and that he could meet my real needs in amazing ways.

SOURCE: www.GiveWithJoy.org - True Generosity Stories

REFLECT/DISCUSS

Can you recall a time when you experienced God's crazy math and saw the Lord provide in unexpected ways?

PRAYER

Heavenly Father, help us realize that you are the owner of all things and that you have many ways you can provide for us. AMEN

DAY 19
The secret

2 COR. 9:7   *God loves a cheerful giver.*

Would you like to be a more generous person than you ever dreamed possible? Would you like to always have money and time to share with your church, ministries, and the needy? Would you like giving to be the highest financial priority in your life? Would you like to be a cheerful giver—even a hilarious giver? Would you like to experience God's love in amazing ways? This is ALL possible!

I believe there is one major secret that must be learned and practiced to become a generous, sharing, caring, joyful, cheerful, and hilarious giver. The secret is learning to "set aside" unto the Lord resources and time to give. Once we start setting aside money to give, based on God's provisions and blessings in our lives, we will constantly have money to share. Once we set aside time each week, each month, and each year to intentionally serve the Lord, we will be amazed at the opportunities God will lead us to in order to be used by him to bless others.

Putting up an imaginary wall to separate what we live on versus what we give on will free us to be incredibly generous with everything that is set aside for the Lord.

If we don't set aside resources and time to give, every request for help will make us feel tight-fisted, pressured, and sometimes even angry. But when we intentionally set aside finances, time, and things for the Lord, we will actually be excited and prayerfully look for God-given opportunities to give, share, and serve. This "set aside" secret will truly change our lives and allow us to live open-handed in a tight-fisted world.

A businessman's #1 priority

> *If you learn to faithfully set aside money and time for God, God will faithfully show you where to give it.*
>
> Brian Kluth,
> Author &
> Speaker

A number of years ago, while serving at a Christian camp, I met Steve who was part-owner in a family business. Steve was one of the most generous people I'd ever met, and he gave many large donations to the camp. The family business went through some problems, and Steve moved to another state to start a new company. I visited him in his new offices, and I knew his young company was struggling. During our meeting, he made a commitment to give another generous gift to the camp. I asked him, "How can you afford to do that?" He told me in his career he had made a lot of money and lost a lot of money. The only thing that remained constant was he always "set aside" the first part of all the money he received to give to the Lord. Regardless of the ups and downs of the economy and his business, Steve always instructed his accountant that their top financial priority was to faithfully set aside money so he could consistently and generously keep giving to his church and the Lord's work.

SOURCE: www.GiveWithJoy.org - True Generosity Stories

REFLECT/DISCUSS

Why do you think the secret of "setting aside" money and time for the Lord will allow someone to always be generous?

PRAYER

Heavenly Father, help us to faithfully set aside resources and time, then show us where to share it. AMEN

DAY 20
What if?

They faithfully brought in their contributions, tithes and dedicated gifts.

Over the years, I have met people who told me they don't give regularly, but only give when God leads them. While I believe and practice the idea of giving when and where God leads, this isn't the whole picture of what he desires for us in our generosity journey.

Without people systematically giving to their local church, missions, missionaries, ministries, and to the needy, God's workers and work in the world would be seriously hindered.

Having been a pastor and missionary, I can share that it was the faithful givers who gave every week or month, no matter how large or small an amount, who allowed the ministries I was involved in to flourish.

What if your employer decided to only give paychecks when he felt led to give them? What if a mother decided to only make dinner when she felt led to cook? What if a schoolteacher, government worker, or shop owner only came to work when they felt led to do so? What if we only went to school or work on the days we felt led? These choices would lead to chaos and confusion everywhere! Our world would come crashing down around us if everyone decided they would only do things when they felt led to do so. Our lives and choices are not to be built on our feelings but on our desire to be faithful to what we know God wants us to be doing.

The truth is God wants all of us to learn to become systematic, faithful, consistent, and generous givers based on the financial provisions and blessings he brings into our lives. Our world and God's work depends on it!

SYSTEMATICALLY give

5

89-year-old widow starts giving

> *Giving 10% is the training wheels of learning to trust God. Giving allows us to experience God as our true Provider.*
>
> Brian Kluth,
> Speaker
> & Author

A friend sent me an email about his 89-year-old mother. She phoned to tell him she stopped giving 10% or more of her income to the Lord years earlier because she was on a fixed income. She was afraid if she started giving again she wouldn't have enough to live on. But after reading my *40-Day Journey to a More Generous Life* Bible devotional she decided to make a spiritual decision to start giving again. Within a few days, she got a call from her pastor inviting her to go on a church retreat, and the church offered to cover all the costs. The next day, she went to her bank to get some spending money for the retreat and the bank teller told her: "You don't need to withdraw any money. Because your 90th birthday is coming up, we have decided to give you a birthday present of $100 in cash!" A little while later, she received a letter from a community group to let her know she had been chosen to receive a $500 grant to help pay her utility bills. After she began giving again, she was amazed at the unexpected provision she received from the Lord.

SOURCE: www.GiveWithJoy.org - True Generosity Stories

REFLECT/DISCUSS

Have you ever been unfaithful, fearful, or tight-fisted when it comes to giving to God? Why do you think this is? What can you learn from this woman's story?

PRAYER

Heavenly Father, help us to overcome our fears, our past failures, and to become faithful givers to your work. Please let us see and experience your provisions in our life. AMEN

DAY 21
Head giving and heart giving

MAL 3:8

*"Will a mere mortal rob God? Yet you rob me.
"But you ask, 'How are we robbing you?'
"In tithes and offerings."*

Do you know what the difference is between the words tithes and offerings?

The word *tithe* referred to the systematic, intentional, and consistent giving of the first 10% of something to God. It is a spiritual decision you make by using your head. You calculate the value of something you have received, and you give the first 10% to the Lord.

But giving offerings in the Bible is different. Offerings were often associated with God moving in your heart to give something you possessed. In Exodus 25, God told Moses to "tell the Israelites to bring me an offering. You are to receive the offering for me from everyone whose heart prompts them to give."

A tithe was expected from each of the Israelites, and to not give 10% was considered stealing from God. But offerings were completely voluntary and were based on God prompting someone's heart to give.

I have discovered God prompting people to give offerings often centers on things they possess that are to be given to specific person or project. It's not about giving a percentage of something—it's about giving whatever you might possess. The Israelites gave offerings to building projects. Early Christians gave offerings for the needy by selling houses and land. In my family's generosity journey, God has prompted us to give away savings, vehicles, clothing, use of our home, materials, products, and much more. I believe God wants each of us to practice both faithful, systematic head-giving AND joyful, spontaneous heart-giving to the Lord.

SPONTANEOUSLY give as the LORD leads you

Being part of God's miracle

Early in his career, Darren Whitehead worked for a small Christian radio station. He received a modest salary and a company car. He tried to sell his own car, but nobody was interested. Darren started to pray God would sell his car, and he sensed God asking him, "What will you do with the money if I sell your car?" "Spend it!" was his first thought. But in his mind he then saw a vivid image of a co-worker's family who were having a tough time financially. So Darren said, "God, if you sell my car, I'll give a sizeable portion to this family." A number then popped into his head that was far more than anything he'd ever given before. Soon afterwards, someone bought his car. He went to the bank, cashed the check, and put a wad of money in an envelope. That night he drove to his co-worker's house, stuffed the envelope in the mailbox, and dashed back to his car. The next day at work, the co-worker had a group of people gathered around him, and he was sobbing. He held up the envelope and said, "Darren, look at this, look what God gave me. It is a miracle!" Darren thought to himself: "Yes, God did give him that money, and I got to be part of God's miracle!"

SOURCE: Darren Whitehead from Willow Creek Church and *Igniting a Life of Generosity*

REFLECT/DISCUSS

Can you recall a time when you have been on the receiving end or the giving end of one of God's miracles?

PRAYER

Heavenly Father, help us to be part of a miracle in other people's lives. AMEN

DAY 22
Who is at your doorstep?

LUKE 16:19-20

There was a certain rich man who was splendidly clothed and who lived each day in luxury. At his door lay a diseased beggar named Lazarus.

Two people lived on the same street. One had everything he needed, wanted, and more. The other truly had nothing. Both died. The unnamed rich man went to hell and Lazarus, the poor man, went to Heaven. As the rich man complained about his fate, Abraham said to him, "During your lifetime you had everything you wanted, and Lazarus had nothing."

The rich man probably passed by Lazarus every day, but was too self-absorbed with his wants, worries, and wealth to notice the beggar hoping for some crumbs from the rich man's table so he could have something to eat. Lazarus was sick, poor, and dying. He needed someone's loving hand to help him, but the only attention he received was from the dogs that came by and licked his sores.

Let's face it, none of us feel comfortable being confronted with the faces of the truly needy. Our typical response is to look away, turn away, walk away, or drive away as quickly as possible. But is it possible God's plan might be that he wants to lead us to stop sometimes. To look into their eyes and find ways we—and maybe even others—can help meet their felt or real needs? Sometimes people need a hand-out, but other times they need a hand up to get their life turned around. Can we ask God to show us how to move past our self-absorbed wants and worries so we can show God's love with a person or family in need? Our crumbs, compassion and caring might be all that is needed to change someone's life and our eternity.

SIMPLIFY your life to become more generous

43

Two miles from a millionaire's mansion

In the TV show, *The Secret Millionaire*, a wealthy person is taken to a needy community, given an old car to drive, a rundown house to stay in, and $50 cash to live on for a week. This person then finds organizations and ministries that are truly helping people, and offers to volunteer their time for a day without anyone knowing their millionaire status. At the end of the week, they reveal their true identity and give out five- or six-figure donations. One millionaire was surprised when she was taken only 2 miles from her mansion to a needy area of her city she barely knew existed. She wept throughout the week as she worked with need-meeting organizations serving pregnant teens, the homeless, runaways, drug addicts, and people with medical problems. All of this was happening only 2 miles from her house and she never knew it. At the end of the week, she tearfully and joyfully shared some of her wealth with shocked and surprised leaders, staff and volunteers to help them in their important work.

SOURCE: *The Secret Millionaire TV Show*

REFLECT/DISCUSS

Where is a needy area within a few miles of you? What organizations serving the needy can you or your group learn more about or help for at least a day?

PRAYER

Heavenly Father, open our eyes to the needy at our doorstep and the need-meeting groups in our community and world. Help us to share our time and treasure with them. AMEN

DAY 23
The truth of God and the lies of the enemy

LUKE 14:33 *No one can become my disciple without giving up everything for me.*

What is the real test to determine if a Christian is going to live generously with their time, talent, treasure, and things?

Jesus puts it all on the line when he says we cannot be his disciple without giving up everything for him. When we first hear these words of Jesus, the enemy of our soul makes us sometimes think that if we follow Jesus we will immediately have to leave everything to serve God on the other side of the world or that we will become destitute—without any money, shelter, clothing, food, friends, or family. But these are distorted lies from the enemy. The reality is when we yield 100% of our life and resources to the Lord, he will guide us and provide for us. No earthly thing will be more sacred and precious to us than God's love and leadership in our lives. We will understand everything on earth is only temporary—possessions, positions, and provisions only belong to us for a short time. Our life and all we have will be at the Lord's disposal to use as he sees fit as we live open-handed in this tight-fisted world. And while we are living this life of complete surrender, God will take care of us in amazing ways.

In Matthew 19:27, Peter says to the Lord, "We've given up everything to follow you. What will we get?" Jesus replies, "Everyone who has given up houses or brothers or sisters or father or mother or children or property, for my sake, will receive a hundred times as much in return and will inherit eternal life." If we submit all we are and all we have to the Lord, he will provide for us in this life and reward us in the next.

$1-a-year salary + God = enough

Conversion is a complete surrender to Jesus. It's a willingness to do what he wants you to do.

Billy Sunday,
Evangelist
1862-1935

For 10 years I was the pastor at a wonderful church. I taught my congregation about how God provides and how he wants us to learn to live generously. They believed that since my teaching was so helpful to them, if they shared me with the rest of the world, then God could use my life to bless and encourage millions of people to trust God as their provider and to live generously. So they commissioned me to become a "Generosity Minister-at-Large" to the body of Christ. This new position came with a $1-a-year salary, medical care for my family, and the faith that God would provide for my family and ministry through churches and people

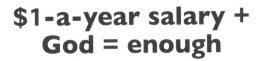

ordering my generosity materials, speaking engagements, and God's creative provisions. Every Monday morning since, I've never known how God was going to meet the needs of the coming week. Yet week after week, God has been providing for my family and this global generosity ministry. I have discovered that *$1 a year + God = ENOUGH.*

SOURCE: www.GiveWithJoy.org - True Generosity Stories

REFLECT/DISCUSS

Do you believe you have fully surrendered yourself and all you have to the Lord? If not, what is holding you back?

PRAYER

Heavenly Father, we want to follow you fully. Help us to surrender all we are and all we have without holding anything back. AMEN

DAY 24
Lighting up the darkness

PS 119:105   *Your word is a lamp for my feet,*
a light on my path.

Have you ever tried to walk around in pitch black darkness? Did you bump into things, stumble, or trip because you couldn't see?

Years ago, I worked at a Christian camp and conference ministry that was located in the middle of thousands of acres of forests and lakes. Sometimes when I would come out of the office after working late, it would be so dark I couldn't see my hands even if I lifted them up in front of my face. So, I would have to walk very carefully down the steps holding tightly onto the railing. I would then have to put my hands out in front of me and very carefully walk in the direction of where I thought I left my car in the parking lot. After walking slowly into the parking lot, my hands would eventually touch a metal object, and I would realize I had found my car. I would then slowly feel my way around the car and finally find the door latch to open the door, get in, turn on the lights and drive home.

But do you know what? When I had a flashlight, I would confidently step out of the office door into the darkness, shine my light and quickly go down the stairs, walk confidently over to the car, get in and drive home. What was the difference? I had a light that helped me see.

The Bible says in Proverbs 4:19 that men stumble around in the darkness, and they don't even know what makes them stumble. The reason is they have no light to guide them. God's Word can be our light in the darkness when it comes to our finances, possessions, living generously, and helping others. We can walk confidently, even with darkness all around us, because we have God's Word to show us the right way.

A communist learns God is the owner and provider

Darkness cannot drive out darkness -- only light can do that.

Martin Luther King Jr.,
Minister &
Civil Rights Leader
1929-1968

I was teaching a seminar on what the Bible says about finances to Christians in Eastern Europe. After the seminar, a man came up and told me how much the teaching had helped everyone. He said that during the 70 years of communism in his country, people were told the communist government owned everything. Government would provide for everyone and meet their needs. He went on to say that when communism fell, people came from other countries and said capitalism – when people are the owners of everything and they have to provide for their own needs—was the way to go. He said this teaching helped some people, but not everyone. He then said to me "Today, I learned the truth. God is the owner of everything, he is our true provider and we must learn to faithfully manage and generously share whatever God gives us".

SOURCE: www.GiveWithJoy.org - True Generosity Stories

REFLECT/DISCUSS

What is one way that God has used this devotional to shine light in the darkness for you when it comes to finances, possessions, living generously, and helping others?

PRAYER

Heavenly Father, thank you for the light of your Word. Thanks for lighting up our darkness so we can walk confidently and securely in this life. Help us to not only live by your Light, but to share it with those who are in darkness. AMEN

DAY 25
#1 way to have your needs met

MATT 6:33

Seek the Kingdom of God above all else, and live righteously, and he will give you everything you need.

The Lord tells us if we live for him every day then we will see him provide for our needs. Regardless of what is happening at our place of employment or in the economy, this promise was true thousands of years ago, is still true today, and will always be true in the future.

The question is not if can God provide for us, but do we have the faith to believe and act on the Matthew 6:33 promise?

We should never get up and go to work every day just to get a pay check or go to school just to get good grades. Instead, we need to get up every day to serve God—to seek first his kingdom and his righteousness in our daily activities. When we do this, God promises to meet our needs in a way we will see his provisions in our life.

Paychecks and school tests come and go, but God remains forever. God's ways, will, and work must be our focus each day wherever we are and whatever we find ourselves doing. Ephesians 2:10 tells us, "We are God's workmanship, created in Christ Jesus to do good works, which God prepared in advance for us to do". This encouragement is not just for pastors and missionaries—though they get to practice this truth—but it is for every one of us. We have all been created specifically by God to do good works he has planned for us. Many of these good works will happen in the midst of our daily work, activities, and relationships. And when we live for God each day, we will see him meet our daily needs in amazing ways as our loving Heavenly Father.

SEE what God has provided

Factory worker's $500 miracle bonus

Our three-year-old church had a chance to buy a $2 million building for only $500,000. The catch was we had to come up with the money in 90 days. I told everyone in the church to be watching for unexpected financial blessings in their life during this time. A factory worker named Mike told me he thought it was foolish to tell people to look for unexpected monies so they could generously give to this miracle project. But the very next week, his foreman called him into the office and gave him an envelope. Mike thought it was a pink slip saying he was being laid off. Instead, it was a $500 bonus for his good work. Mike couldn't believe it; he had never heard of anyone getting a bonus before. He joyfully gave the $500 to the 90-day building fund project. With Mike's unexpected bonus and many other gifts, on the 90th day, we all rejoiced when we were able to purchase the $2 million building for only $500,000.

SOURCE: www.GiveWithJoy.org - True Generosity Stories

REFLECT/DISCUSS

Why do you think that seeking first the kingdom of God will help us experience our own needs being met?

PRAYER

Heavenly Father, thank you that your Word is true and that your promises never fail. Thank you for meeting our needs when we live for you each day. AMEN

DAY 26
Becoming Jesus with skin on

DEUT. 26:12 *When you have finished setting aside a tenth of all your produce in the third year, the year of the tithe, you shall give it to the Levite, the foreigner, the fatherless and the widow, so that they may eat in your towns and be satisfied..*

God's servants and the needy God puts in your life truly need your faithful and generous help. Pastors, teachers, church staff, missionaries, and ministry workers are dependent on the faithful and generous gifts of God's people. Needy people God puts within our gaze or reach can be blessed by us as we become "Jesus with skin on" in their lives.

God's Word reminds us we need to actively set aside resources to give to God's servants and to the needy. If we intentionally and faithfully set aside resources from the financial blessings God gives us, we will be amazed at how generous we can become. As we set resources aside, we will joyfully and prayerfully look for ways to share with others. The purpose of our sharing will be to bless others, meet some of their needs, bring joy to their hearts, and praise to God on their lips.

Sometimes our setting aside will come from systematically giving from our income and financial blessings. Other times it will come from sacrificial giving by giving something up to be able to give more. In the story on the next page, a little girl gave the money she was going to use for ice cream to help purchase a camp for children in Hong Kong. Once we set aside resources "unto the Lord" he can direct it, use it, and multiply it to bless other people through our lives to help us become "Jesus with skin on."

In my own generosity journey, this principle of actively "setting aside" resources to give has allowed me to joyfully and generously give thousands of dollars to God's work, God's servants, and the needy.

SET ASIDE resources to give

4

Little girl's $1 buys multi-million-dollar camp

I heard a missionary tell an amazing story of a child's generosity. John Bechtel, a missionary in Hong Kong, wanted to start a Christian camp to reach children and adults for Christ. A multi-million-dollar orphanage and school became available. He made an offer to purchase the property and then traveled around the world to raise the millions he would need. But no one was willing to help, and he returned to Hong Kong discouraged. Then one day he got a letter from a young girl. Inside the letter was $1 and a note saying she had set aside her ice cream money in order to be able to send it to John to help buy the camp. This was all the money he received. John prayed and took the girl's $1 and letter to the sellers who decided to accept it as full payment for the property! This camp has since welcomed more than one million people through its doors and over 100,000 have accepted Christ.

SOURCE: www.GiveWithJoy.org - True Generosity Stories

REFLECT/DISCUSS

Have you ever gone without something in order to be able to set aside money to give a sacrificial gift to the Lord's work? What is something you could live without—for a while or forever—in order to help you be able to set aside funds to be more generous?

PRAYER

Heavenly Father, help us to live more simply so others can simply live. AMEN

DAY 27
Generosity explosion

2 CHR 31:5,12 *The people responded immediately and generously with the first of their crops and grain, new wine, olive oil, money, and everything else…a tithe of all they owned. They faithfully brought in their contributions, tithes and dedicated gifts..*

Sometimes people become lazy in their giving to the Lord's work. Over time they get caught up in living their own lives and drift away from being faithful, systematic, and generous givers to God's work. They become consumed by their own worries, wants, or wealth and give God's work little or no priority in their lives.

This was the case when King Hezekiah came to the throne in Israel. The Bible says he was good, right and true before the Lord his God. God used Hezekiah to start a generosity movement among his people. He called, commanded, and challenged God's people to do what was right in the eyes of the Lord with regard to their giving. He told them they should give the portion due to God's servants, and they should devote themselves to following God's Word.

The results were nothing short of miraculous. People responded positively and immediately—they began bringing their first fruits, tithes, contributions, and gifts. For four months in a row, giving exploded and the offerings had to be piled up in great heaps. More people even had to be recruited to count and organize all the offerings given.

Sometimes we all get off track in life, and we need God to raise up a leader to remind us to do what is right in our giving. When we respond positively and immediately, the results will be amazing and miraculous for all to see.

SYSTEMATICALLY give

African family saves children from going blind

> *Do all the good you can, in all the ways you can, at all the times you can, as long as you can.*
>
> John Wesley, Pastor and Founder of the Methodist Movement 1703-1791

While in Africa, I met a man who raised his 6 children on $10 a month. He told me children in his village were going blind because of a disease that could be stopped with medicine that only cost 50 cents. He began to pray and ask God to send a rich person to help, but no one ever came. As he kept praying, the Lord told him he should give the money to buy the medicine. But with 6 children and only a $10 a month salary, he couldn't see how he could do this. But his family prayed and decided that every month they would sacrifice and systematically set aside money to buy medicine for one of the children in their village. When I spoke with him, they had been doing this for 7 years and had saved 84 children from going blind. He also shared how God provided for his family in amazing ways. As he and his family sought to do what they could to help others, God sought to help them.

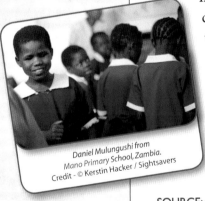

Daniel Mulungushi from Mano Primary School, Zambia.
Credit - © Kerstin Hacker / Sightsavers

SOURCE: www.GiveWithJoy.org - True Generosity Stories

REFLECT/DISCUSS

Where in the world is there a child or a ministry you know that serves children who could benefit from your systematic help every month?

PRAYER

Heavenly Father, if we have a pulse we have a purpose. Help us to realize that one of our purposes in life is to systematically be of help to others. AMEN

DAY 28
Extravagant giving

MARK 14:3 — *On the first day of every week, each one of you should put aside money as you have been blessed.*

The beautiful aroma must have immediately filled the air as this woman poured expensive perfume on Jesus' head. We know it wasn't some cheap-smelling, inexpensive perfume because the Bible says it could have been sold for more than a year's wages. A year's wages! That's a lot of money!

Some people in the room complained and said the perfume should have been sold and the money given to the poor. But Jesus did not condemn the woman. Instead, he commended her for what she had done. Was the real concern of those grumbling for the poor or for themselves? When people are around someone who gives an extravagant gift to Jesus, it can make them feel uncomfortable and defensive. They instinctively know they would never do something so extreme and radical.

The generous gift of perfume from this woman likely represented many years of work, hopes, and dreams. And yet she was willing to gladly, gratefully, and generously pour this expensive gift of perfume onto Jesus' head in front of others. This extravagant gift wasn't done in secret, but instead was done in the open for all to see (and smell)!

Our private and public Spirit-led giving, when done spontaneously and generously, can be a pleasing aroma to God. While other tight-fisted and grumbling people might be uncomfortable with our extravagant generosity, we can learn to be open-handed like this woman to honor and worship Jesus because we love him so much.

Christmas: Whose birthday is it?

One year when Christmas was approaching, my children kept telling me all the gifts they wanted. I spontaneously asked them one day, "Whose birthday are we celebrating?" They replied, "Jesus." I asked, "Well, who should get the biggest presents?" They said, "Jesus, but he's not here!" This got me thinking, and when the time came to open our Christmas presents, my wife and I gave each of our children (and ourselves) an envelope with a large amount of cash inside. Also in each envelope was a list we had prayerfully put together with the names of widows, ministers, missionaries, ministries, and needy families whom my children knew. We then explained to our children that when we help the least, the lost, the lonely and God's leaders, it is like giving Christmas presents to Jesus. Each of us then had to decide who we wanted to give to and how much we were going to give. Everyone then shared their giving decisions with the family. Afterwards, we opened our presents which were worth only a fraction of the money we had just given away. This tradition continues and every Christmas Jesus gets the biggest presents!

SOURCE: www.GiveWithJoy.org - True Generosity Stories

REFLECT/DISCUSS

What are your thoughts about the idea of giving Jesus the "biggest presents" at Christmas? How could this practice positively impact your family?

PRAYER

Heavenly Father, help us to get excited about giving presents to Jesus by helping the least, the lonely, the lost, and God's leaders. AMEN

DAY 29
De-accumulate

1 CHR 29:2-5 *King David said, "I now give my personal treasures of gold and silver for the temple of my God."*

Over his lifetime, King David accumulated many things. Eventually, he realized that all he accumulated had to be de-accumlated.

Just like David, we all go through various seasons of life, and we will naturally accumulate things along the way. But as we move through each season, what are we going to do with all the things we have accumulated? The need for baby/toddler things will pass as our children get older. Teen possessions will no longer be needed as children become adults. At the start of each new season of life (or every year), we must all learn to intentionally de-clutter our lives and de-accumulate the things we no longer use. Some things can be passed along to family and loved ones who can use them or who would appreciate having them. Other things can be sold or discarded. Some of our possessions can be used to further God's work at our church, in missions, or among the needy.

I am sure King David's family members received many nice gifts from him over the years. But David was also a man after God's heart. In his later years, he decided to simplify his life and intentionally de-accumulate. God moved in his heart to generously give to the temple building project that would bless and benefit many people for generations to come.

In 1 Timothy 6, we are told to use our wealth for good and to be rich in good deeds. Like King David, by doing this we will honor God, store up treasure in heaven, bless others, and live a joyful life in the here and now. Eventually we must all let go of things we have accumulated at each stage or season of our lives. Wise people de-accumulate intentionally for the glory of God and the benefit of others.

Elderly woman's baby furniture

One Sunday I was guest preaching at a church. I talked about the importance of de-accumulating things we no longer used or needed. I even jokingly said I thought some people were going to go up to heaven feet first because they would be trying to hold onto all their possessions. After the message, an elderly woman stormed up to me. She was visibly upset. She said, "I can't believe you told me to throw all my things away." I told her that's not what I said and asked her what she was referring to. She told me she had beautiful baby furniture in her attic. I then asked her how old she was, and she replied, "88!" I shared with her that I knew a young couple in her church who had very little money and were about to have their first baby. I suggested she let them use or have the furniture rather than leaving it sitting in the attic. The light bulb went on, her eyes began to sparkle, and she became so excited about helping this young couple by sharing what she had but no longer needed.

SOURCE: www.GiveWithJoy.org - True Generosity Stories

REFLECT/DISCUSS

Are there things you have you no longer use or need? Who could you pass them on to? Is there anything special you have you can release to advance God's work?

PRAYER

Heavenly Father, teach us to live in light of eternity. Help us to de-accumulate things we no longer use or need in a way that glorifies you and benefits others. AMEN

DAY 30
& NEXT STEPS

Dear Christian friend:

We are living in a world where the walls of our economy are cracking because they are on shaky ground. We need to return to rebuilding our lives on the foundation of God's Word.

In the early chapters of the book of Nehemiah, God used Nehemiah to lead God's people to rebuild the broken walls of Jerusalem. Then in the 9th and 10th chapter, God used Nehemiah to rebuild the broken down walls of people's faith. He called them to put God first in their lives, their finances, and their generosity. As part of this call, he asked them to sign a spiritual covenant—"We are making a solemn promise and putting it in writing"—to indicate their desire to honor God afresh in their lives. Haggai was also used by God to help people "consider their ways" and give God first place in their lives.

Like it was in the days of Nehemiah and Haggai, I believe that in our generation we need the people of God to make a fresh, personal promise to honor God in our lives, finances, and generosity. I invite you to sign (and even have two witnesses sign) the following personal or family spiritual covenant to indicate your desire to honor God with your life and all he entrusts to you for the rest of your life.

☐ **YES** I want to experience God as my provider, and I want to become a generous person for the rest of my life. I willingly join this Generosity Pledge Movement happening for the glory of God in my generation.

It is my desire, with God's help, to:

1 SUBMIT myself and all I have to the LORD
2 STUDY the Scriptures on finances and generosity
3 SEE what God has provided in my life
4 SET ASIDE resources to give
5 SYSTEMATICALLY give
6 SPONTANEOUSLY give as the LORD leads me
7 SIMPLIFY my life to be even more generous.

Date: _____

Your signature(s): _____

Signature(s) of any participating children: _____

_____

Witnesses: _____

_____

Possible "next steps" in your generosity journey
to excel in the grace of giving:

- *Fill out* the PRACTICAL WORKSHEET on sharing your Time Talent, Treasure, Things *(page 62)*.
- *Look through* the articles and resources in the BONUS MATERIALS *(pages 61 to 74)*.
- *Sign up* for the FREE 40-Day **www.GiveWithJoy.org** eDevotional with daily Bible readings and audio teachings.
- *Sign up* for the **www.GenerousYou.com** 21-Day Giving Challenge.
- *Look into* **www.GodIsYourProvider.com** Resources.

BONUS MATERIALS
TABLE OF CONTENTS

PRACTICAL WORKSHEET

As you seek to live out the **7 KEYS** of the **Generosity Pledge** movement, write down some ideas or specific ways you can be more generous with the following items for the glory of God and the benefit of others:

Sharing your TIME

Work day or school day: _____

Weekends and days off: _____

Holidays: _____

Vacation days: _____

Free time: _____

Other: _____

Sharing your TALENT

Skills/abilities: _____

Hobbies/interests: _____

Education/training: _____

Sports/recreation: _____

Other: _____

Sharing your TREASURE

Main income(s): _____

Extra income(s): _____

Investments: _____

Inheritance/estate: _____

Insurance: _____

Business: _____

Savings: _____

Other: _____

Sharing your THINGS

Home: _____

Possessions: _____

Property: _____

Vehicles: _____

Equipment: _____

Other: _____

GROUP DISCUSSION
QUESTIONS

Watch this week's discussion-starter video
at www.GenerosityPledge.org

DAY

2 Why do you think giving yourself to God is the most important step in learning to become a generous person?

3 If someone asked you how much money you would need to have financial freedom, what amount would you say? Why would learning to look to God as your true provider be more valuable than lots of money in the bank?

4 If God is truly bigger than a paycheck, what are some ways you have seen him bring provisions into your life recently?

5 How do you think looking back each week, writing down all of God's provisions, and setting aside money as a thank-you offering to God would help you be more generous?

6 What are some of the most vivid recollections you have about your personal giving or your family's giving to God?

7 Why do you think God can use the faith of little children to accomplish big things for God's glory? Why is it important for you to cultivate childlike faith in your giving?

8 Would you be willing to pray and, with God's help, determine how much is "enough"? If God gave you extra money beyond this amount, how would you want to use it for God's work?

GROUP DISCUSSION
QUESTIONS

Watch this week's discussion-starter video
at www.GenerosityPledge.org

DAY

9 Why do you think money and material possessions hold such an attraction for most people? What can you learn from the lives of William Borden and King Tut?

10 1 Peter 5:7 tells us to "cast all of our cares upon him because he cares for us." What is something that is troubling you? How can you better use the time and energy you spend worrying to instead worship God in this matter?

11 List some of the available time, talents, treasure, and things that God has given you. What is a way that some of these things could be used for the Lord and for others?

12 If you have an intentional plan for setting aside 10% or more of your financial blessings for God's work, what is that plan? If you haven't done this yet, what could you do to start?

13 If someone looked over your calendar and financial records, who and what would they say is important to you?

14 Whether someone is rich or poor, why do you think possessions become such an attraction and/or distraction for people? Why can't possessions bring lasting happiness? Why can't possessions bring lasting happiness??

15 Name a few of your most prized possessions, proven skills/abilities, available time, or stored-up resources. Have you ever fully yielded these things to God?

GROUP DISCUSSION
QUESTIONS

Watch this week's discussion-starter video
at www.GenerosityPledge.org

DAY	
16	The Apostle Paul says we are to live for God each day. Albert Einstein says we are to live for others. How do you think these two things work together, like the wings of a bird in flight?
17	What are the tangible financial, material, and other provisions God has blessed you with? What is your plan to systematically share these provisions?
18	Can you recall a time when you experienced God's crazy math and saw the Lord provide in unexpected ways?
19	Why do you think the secret of "setting aside" money and time for the Lord will allow someone to always be generous?
20	Have you ever been unfaithful, fearful, or tight-fisted when it comes to giving to God? Why do you think this is? What can you learn from this woman's story?
21	Can you recall a time when you have been on the receiving end or the giving end of one of God's miracles?
22	Where is a needy area within a few miles of you? What organizations serving the needy can you or your group learn more about or help for at least a day?

DAY

23 Do you believe that you have fully surrendered yourself and all you have to the Lord? If not, what is holding you back?

24 What is one way that God has used this devotional to shine light in the darkness for you when it comes to finances, possessions, living generously, and helping others?

25 Why do you think that seeking first the kingdom of God will help us experience our own needs being met?

26 Have you ever gone without something in order to be able to set aside money to give a sacrificial gift to the Lord's work? What is something you could live without—for a while or forever—in order to help you be able to set aside funds to be more generous?

27 Where in the world is there a child or a ministry you know that serves children who could benefit from your systematic help every month?

28 What are your thoughts about the idea of giving Jesus the "biggest presents" at Christmas? How could this practice positively impact your family?

29 Are there things you have that you no longer use or need? Who could you pass them on to? Is there anything special you have that you can release to advance God's work?

God's desire is for Christians to learn to...

Over 100+ Bible verses—check'em out and check'em off!

☐ *Give Generously*
2 Ch 31:5, 1 Ch 29:14-17,
1 Tim 6:17-19, Philemon 1:6

☐ *Give Systematically*
Dt 14:22, Gen 28:16-22,
Prov 3:9-10, Lev 27:30-31

☐ *Give Spontaneously*
1 Ch 29:14, Ex 35:21-29, 36:3

☐ *Give Radically*
Acts 2:44-45, 4:32-37,
1 Kgs 17:7-16, 19:19-21

☐ *Give Reverently*
Mt 2:11, Dt 14:23, Ex 34:26,
Mal 1:6-9, Lv 22:20, Rev 5:12

☐ *Give Freely*
Mt 10:8, Prov 11:24,
Ezra 1:4-6, 2 Ch 31:14

☐ *Give Humbly*
Deut 8:18, Ps 112:9,
Mt 6:1-3, 1 Ch 29:14

☐ *Give Cheerfully*
2 Corinthians 9:7

☐ *Give Proportionally*
1 Cor 16:2, Deut 16:17,
Exodus 35:5, Ezra 2:69

☐ *Give Willingly*
2 Cor 8:12, 1 Chron 29:6,
Exodus 35:21-22, Dt 15:10

☐ *Give Joyfully*
2 Chron 24:10, 29:36,
2 Corinthians 8:2

☐ *Give Regularly*
Deut 16:16, 1 Cor 16:2,
Neh 10:35-39, Num 18:28-29

☐ *Give Thoughtfully*
Hag 1:3-11, 2 Cor 9:6-7

☐ *Give Faithfully*
Lu 16:9-11, Dt 14:27,
2 Ch 31:4-8, 1 Cor 4:2

☐ *Give Expectantly*
Lu 6:38, 12:33, Phil 4:19,
Mal 3:8-10, 2 Cor 9

☐ *Give Eternally*
Mt 6:19-20, 1 Tim 6:19,
Mk 10:21, Heb 11:13-16

☐ *Give Extravagantly*
Jn 12:1-8, Mk 12:41-44,
1 Chron 29:2-9, Ex 35

☐ *Give Thankfully*
1 Tim 6:6-10, Ps 50:14

Romans 15:4 says,
**"Everything that was written
in the past was written
to teach us."**

Source: Pastor Brian Kluth, Founder of the www.GenerosityPledge.org Movement

ONLINE RESOURCES

GENEROSITY WEBSITES

- GenerosityPledge.org
- GiveWithJoy.org
- GenerousLife.org
- GenerousGiving.org
- GenerousYou.com
- NationalChristian.com
- TheGathering.com
- StewardshipMinistries.org
- AcceptableGift.org
- GenerosityMovement.org
- EPM.org
- StewardshipCouncil.net
- IssacharInitiative.org
- GiveToGenerosity.org
- KardiaPlanning.com
- ExcellenceInGiving.com
- JunkyCarClub.com
- Royal Treasure.org

GIVING WEBSITES

- ECFA.org
- GiveToGenerosity.org
- GuideStar.org
- MinistryWatch.com
- WallWatchers.com
- NetworkforGood.org
- CharityNavigator.org
- Give.org
- iDonate.com
- MinistrySpotlight.org
- ServantMatch.org
- GlobalFast.org

FINANCIAL WEBSITES

- GodIsYourProvider.com
- MyFamilyForms.org
- Compass1.org
- Crown.org
- GoodSenseMinistry.com
- DaveRamsey.com
- KingdomAdvisors.org
- 360FinancialLiteracy.org

- DebtProofLiving.com
- MattAboutMoney.com
- BobMarette.com
- RonBlue.com
- SoundMindInvesting.com
- StewardshipPartners.com
- Christ@Work: fcci-online.org

GENEROSITY WEBSITES FOR PASTORS/CHURCHES

- MAXIMUMgenerosity.org
- GenerousLife.org
- GenerosityPledge.org
- STATEofthePLATE.info
- ChristianStewardshipNetwork.com
- GenerousChurch.com
- StewardshipMinistries.org
- VisionResourcingGroup.com
- GlobalGenerosity.org
- Fulcrumps.com *Planned Giving*
- PlannedGivingMinistries.com
- GenerosityMonk.com
- StewardshipResources.org
- EffectiveStewardship.com
- StewardshipDirect.com
- IntSteward.org
- ChristianityToday.com
- AnnualStewardship.com
- RevolutionInGenerosity.com
- iDonate.com
- StewardshipCouncil.net
- RoyalTreasure.org
- Stewardship.org
- NACBA.net

*Go to **www.Kluth.org** for a list of Capital Campaign Firms*

10 reasons to give 10% or more

As materialism and consumerism have infiltrated our lives in recent decades, many people have drifted from any biblical moorings concerning their Christian giving. Here are 10 biblically based and practical reasons to make giving 10% or more to God's work the highest financial priority in your life.

1 *It is a proven pattern of giving done by Christ's followers for many generations.* In 1899, a bibliography was compiled of books related to systematic Christian giving. There were over 500 books listed in this bibliography from over 100 years ago, demonstrating a long tradition of open-handed giving, and yet many Christians today do not understand the importance of faithful and generous giving. GENESIS 14:17-20, GENESIS 28:16-22, LEVITICUS 27:30, PROVERBS 3:9-10, MALACHI 3:7-15, MATTHEW 23:23

2 *It will give the Lord first place in your life.* If I saw your financial records, I would quickly know who or what you value. By giving the best of what you have to God, you are expressing your allegiance to him. You will grow in your respect for the Lord and will see him working more actively in your life. DEUTERONOMY 14:23, MALACHI 1:6-8

3 *It will bring God's wisdom and order to your finances.* If I get dressed in the morning and get the first button out of place on my shirt, all the rest of the buttons will be messed up. When it comes to finances, the first button to get in place is your giving. When you get this area in order, everything else follows. Giving is also the only known antidote for "affluenza" (the desire for more things), which permeates our world today. MATTHEW 6:19-21, MATTHEW 6:24-34; LUKE 12:16-21, I TIMOTHY 6:6-10, 17-19; ECCLESIASTES 5:10

4 *It will serve as a practical reminder that God is the Owner of everything in your life.* By faithfully giving the Lord 10% or more of all you ever receive, you are actively acknowledging his ownership in your life. As someone once told me, "God owns it all and God loans it all." We are not owners, only temporary possessors and managers of what God entrusts to us during our lifetime. I CHRONICLES 29:11-18, PSALM 24:1-2, PSALM 50:10-12, HAGGAI 2:8

5 *It will allow you to experience God as your Provider.* One of the most amazing things about learning to faithfully give to the Lord is the joy you will expereince when you see God provide for you in creative ways that show his love for you as your Heavenly Father. I KINGS 17, PROVERBS 3:9-10, MALACHI 3:7-15, HAGGAI 1:4-11, HAGGAI 2:15-19; LUKE 6:38, DEUTERONOMY 28, PHILIPPIANS 4:15-19, MARK 12:41-44

6 *It will encourage your spiritual growth and trust in God.* There will be times when you will decide to be a faithful giver of what is in your hand, even when you have no idea how you will make it through the coming day, week, or month. But by going ahead and giving to God, your trust in the Lord will grow, and you will grow in your ability to see him provide. DEUTERONOMY 14:23, PROVERBS 3:5-6, MALACHI 3:8-10, HAGGAI 1:4-11, HAGGAI 2:15-19; 2 CORINTHIANS 8:5

7 *It will ensure you of treasure in heaven.* Jesus encourages you to store up treasure in heaven. The only way to do this is to live generously now. Someone once said, "We can't take it with us, but we can send it on ahead." I TIMOTHY 6:18-19, MATTHEW 6:19-21, HEBREWS 6:10, III JOHN 8, I SAMUEL 30:22

8 *It will strengthen the work and outreach of your local church.* Many churches struggle due to lack of finances. However, when people in a congregation gain a vision of being faithful givers to God at their local church, the whole spirit of a church begins to change—needs are met, people are cared for, more outreach begins to take place, and long-awaited improvements start to happen. God-given momentum builds as people honor the Lord through their giving at church. ACTS 2:42-47, ACTS 4:32; 2 CORINTHIANS 9:12, 13

9 *It will help provide the means to keep your pastor(s) and missionaries in full-time Christian service.* It has always been God's plan that his servants are taken care of by his people. Many pastors and missionaries are struggling financially or are even leaving the ministry because of a lack of adequate finances. Your faithful giving can make sure this doesn't happen among the pastors or missionaries you know. I CORINTHIANS 9:9-11,14; I TIMOTHY 5:17-18, III JOHN 5-8, PHILIPPIANS 4:15-19, GALATIANS 6:6, LUKE 8:3, II KINGS 4:8-10

10 *It will help accomplish needed building projects and renovations.* Some of the most exciting times in the life of a church or ministry occur when facilities are being improved or expanded to help reach more people for Christ. But for building projects to succeed, large and extraordinary gifts are needed. Building projects only happen well with special gifts that are "above and beyond" what people normally give. This usually happens when people make sacrificial gifts or pledges (by going without something so they can give more) or because they give generously from "whatever they have" (including possessions, property, or wealth). 2 CHRONICLES 24:4-14, EXODUS 35,36; II KINGS 12:2-16, EZRA 1:4-6, I CHRONICLES 29:2-19

*Source: Pastor Brian Kluth, Founder of the **www.GenerosityPledge.org** Movement*

Practical advice about giving

By Pastor Brian Kluth, Founder of the www.GenerosityPledge.org Movement

Here is some practical advice for people who have questions, doubts, or fears about faithfully and generously giving to the Lord's work.

If you are NOT a Christian: Don't focus on giving to God at this time—but instead discover and accept what God wants to give you—complete forgiveness, a brand-new start, the power to be good and to do good, help for your problems, guidance from the Bible, the ability to forgive, and a home in heaven. God gives these things to you when you admit that you are a sinner who needs Jesus to be your Savior—because he took the punishment for your sins on the cross. Ask Jesus to come into your life and to be your living Lord and Savior.

For all Christians: Always make it a priority to faithfully support the work of your local church first. Then give special gifts and offerings to other Christian causes, projects, missions, or the needy as God leads you.

If you're fearful about giving 10% or more of your income to the Lord, try a 90-day test: In Malachi 3:10, God invites people to "test"him in the matter of tithing (giving the first 10% of your income to God's work). Therefore, I encourage people to try a 90-day test. Begin giving 10% of your income to the Lord's work and watch and see if God does not begin working in your life in ways you haven't previously experienced. If you regret that decision OR if you feel you never experienced God's divine help in your finances during this time period, then discontinue the test. However, if you experience God's help, joyfully continue giving 10% or more to the Lord's work.

If you want to begin to actively give to God FIRST: Here are four ideas to choose from: **1)** Whenever you get any money, set aside 10% or more to give as the Lord directs. **2)** Whenever you put a deposit in your checkbook, write out the first check(s) to God's work for 10% or more. **3)** If you track your finances through a bookkeeping system or computer program, set up a category for church giving and another one for other Christian causes. Then begin to faithfully set aside 10% or more of your income into these accounts. **4)** If you like to handle your finances electronically, consider using online or electronic giving options to faithfully give 10% or more of your financial blessings to the Lord.

If you are married to a Christian, but the two of you do not agree on how much you should give to the Lord's work: See if your spouse will read through this material and/or listen to some of the Internet messages at www.GiveWithJoy.org or www.GenerosityPledge.org. Then talk and pray together about a mutually agreeable "testing period" concerning your giving 10% or more.

If you are married and your spouse is not a Christian: Identify any money you have freedom to spend (read Luke 8:3) and set aside 10% or more of this money to give to the Lord's work AND/OR show this material to your spouse and see if you can try the 90-day testing period.

If you are trying to decide whether to give off the gross or the net of your income: Pray and ask God what he wants you to do. If he prompts you in your heart to give off the gross amount, go ahead and do this, trusting him with the results. If you don't have a peace about this, begin giving 10% off the net amount for a few months and see what happens. After a few months, if you experience God's creative care in your life, then begin to give 10% or more off your gross income.

If you're wondering about how much to give to your church and how much to give to other places: A good practice I have used is to give 10% of my main source of income to my local church (i.e., my main income goes to support the work of my main source of Christian fellowship and teaching). I then set aside 10% or more of God's extra provisions and financial blessings that he brings into my life so I can give to missionaries, projects, and the needy as the Lord prompts me to give.

If you have children at home: Help your children set up a place where they can set aside "God's portion" of any money they receive (e.g., allowances, work projects, gifts of money, etc.). Have them give at church, to missions, and/or to help people in need.

If you have "fallen behind" in your giving to God's work: If you knowingly or accidentally have fallen behind in your giving to God's work, you will never regret the decision to "get right" in this area. Review your financial records from the past several months and pray about "making up" the amount you have fallen behind. One elderly lady in her 90s I heard about sent a tithe check to the church office with the note, "I want to be prayed up, paid up, and ready to go!"

For more answers to commonly asked questions about giving, go to: www.GenerosityPledge.org

MEDIA INTERVIEWS

Brian Kluth is one of the world's leading generosity experts, and he is frequently interviewed or quoted by publications, news programs, and talk shows—including NBC, CBS, CNN, CBN, FOX, *USA Today*, NPR, AP, *Kiplingers*, Reuters, *Washington Times*, *Wall Street Journal*, newspapers, magazines, and hundreds of radio stations across the country. He is normally available 24/7/365 for live or pre-recorded TV/Radio/Print/Media interviews. He is available to do TV interviews onsite or from studios in Denver or Colorado Springs. For details, go to: *www.BrianKluth.com* and *www.GenerosityPledge.org*

GUEST SPEAKING

Brian Kluth is a popular guest speaker on generosity and financial matters for large churches, conferences, denominations, associations, colleges, seminaries, leadership gatherings, conventions for financial services professionals, fundraising training, and donor events. For details/bookings, go to: *www.BrianKluth.org*.

FOREIGN LANGUAGE TRANSLATIONS

People everywhere can be helped by discovering the truth found in this booklet. As people from around the world have discovered Brian Kluth's generosity devotionals and materials, requests have been received to translate his devotionals and materials into other languages. To find foreign language translations of Brian's materials (and/or to request permission to help translate, distribute, and/or sell his materials), go to: *www.kluth.org/intl.htm*

COPYRIGHT INFORMATION

OTHER RESOURCES
BY BRIAN KLUTH

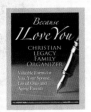

Because I Love You CHRISTIAN LEGACY ORGANIZER *Manual and Seminar DVD*

This manual provides valuable forms for you, your spouse, loved ones, or aging parents. As a minister, Brian discovered that most families do not receive important written information before a loved one passes away. This manual is filled with helpful forms to record information about family history, life lessons, family tree, finances, household items, documents, medical wishes, funeral plans, inheritances, charitable giving, and estate planning. Print or computer versions are available along with online and quantity discounts at *www.MyFamilyForms.org*.

40-Day Journey to a More Generous Life
Bible Devotional and CD

Brian's bestselling 40-Day generosity devotional, videos, and companion materials have been used by thousands of churches to inspire greater generosity in people's lives. This devotional has daily Bible readings, weekly articles and worksheets, and group discussion questions to help people discover God's Word on finances and generosity. There are nearly 500,000 copies in print worldwide, and the devotional is being translated into over 40 foreign languages. Online and quantity discounts are available at *www.MAXIMUMgenerosity.org*.

Experience God as Your Provider: Finding Faith and Financial Stability in Unstable Times *Book, Bookmark, CD*

This material has revolutionized people's thinking and helped them understand that God is bigger than stock markets, job markets, and housing markets. Regardless of what is happening in our economy, God has many creative ways to care for people in the midst of challenging times. These materials are ideal for churches, Sunday School classes, small groups, personal use, or for ministries to give to their supporters. Online and quantity discounts are available at *www.GodIsYourProvider.com*

Generosity Kits for Churches & Ministries
Online or CD

Brian has created online kits of biblically based generosity materials for churches and ministries. Kits include generosity flyers, offertory slides, cartoons, sermon resources, training materials, and videos. To order or to preview, go to: *www.MAXIMUMgenerosity.org*

ORDER 30-DAY DEVOTIONAL

Online: ***www.GenerosityPledge.org*** *- Call 866.935.5884 or 719.302.3383*

SPECIAL! Preview Packet of 10 COPIES & Leaders eGuide: **$29.95**

1 *copy*	**$7.95** *each*	**500-999 copies*	**$3.45** *each*
2-9 *copies*	**$6.95** *each*	**1000-2499 copies*	**$2.95** *each*
10-99 *copies*	**$4.95** *each*	**2499-5000 copies*	**$2.75** *each*
100-499 *copies*	**$3.95** *each*	**Over 5000 copies*	*(Call us)*

Also available for iPad, iBook, iPhone,
Kindle, Nook, PDF, and other readers for $6.95

3 PAYMENT OPTIONS

1) PAY-ON-THE-DAY you place your order
2) 90-DAY-DELAYED PAYMENT *(for 30 or more)*
3) OFFERING-DAY COLLECTION *(for 30 or more)*
We provide these 3 options so EVERY CHURCH
can afford to give the devotional to EVERY FAMILY!

*CUSTOMIZED COVERS FOR JUST $1 MORE!

For orders of 300 or more, we will send you the InDesign files to customize and personalize the 4 pages of the outside/inside covers for just $1 more per booklet.

30-DAY VIDEOS & CAMPAIGN KIT

To increase the effectiveness and positive impact of the 30-Day Devotional, we have created short videos and a CAMPAIGN KIT OF COMPANION MATERIALS. The kit includes 5 VIDEOS (for church services AND/OR SS classes and small groups), sermon helps, banners, posters, online eDevotional, audio teaching files that can be duplicated onto CDs, children's materials, and much more! Price: **$199.95** *(or online discount)*

30-DAY GENEROSITY PLEDGE CARD

Card has tear-off section that can be turned in at the end of the 30 days. Price: **$24.95** *in packets of 50.* Preview at www.GenerosityPledge.org